W9-BNK-590

Sea Otter

by Jen Green

Consultants:

John E. McCosker, PhD
Chair of Aquatic Biology, California Academy of Sciences

Maureen Flannery, MS
Ornithology and Mammalogy Collection Manager, California Academy of Sciences

Wallace J. Nichols, PhD
Research Associate, California Academy of Sciences

BEARPORT
PUBLISHING

New York, New York

Cradlerock Elem. Media Center

Credits

Cover, © Suzi Eszterhas/Minden Pictures/FLPA; 3, © iStockphoto/Thinkstock; 4, © Phillip Colla/Seapics.com; 5, © Milo Burcham/Alaska Stock/Alamy; 6, © Thomas Sbampato/Imagebroker/Alamy; 7TL, © Gail Johnson/Shutterstock; 7TR, © Oceans Image/Photoshot; 7BL, © Ingo Schulz/Imagebroker/Alamy; 7BR, © Four Oaks/Shutterstock; 9, © Bill Rome/Alaska Stock/Alamy; 10TL, © Shutterstock; 10TR, © Marlith/Public Domain; 10BL, © Matthias Breiter/Minden Pictures; 10BR, © iStockphoto/Thinkstock; 11, © Doc White/Seapics.com; 12T, © Chris Arend/Alaska Stock/Alamy; 12B, © Thomas & Pat Leeson/Science Photo Library; 13, © Suzi Eszterhas/Minden Pictures/FLPA; 14T, © Shutterstock; 14B, © iStockphoto/Thinkstock; 15, © Doug Allan/The Image Bank/Getty Images; 16–17, © Milo Burcham/Alaska Stock/Alamy; 18, © Donald M. Jones/Minden Pictures/Getty Images; 19, © Doc White/Seapics.com; 20–21, © Tom Uhlman/Alamy; 22TL, © iStockphoto/Thinkstock; 22TR, © Tomasz Szymanski/Shutterstock; 22CL, © Shutterstock; 22CR, © Dreamstime; 22BL, © iStockphoto; 22BR, © Kevin Schafer/Corbis; 23TL, © Worldswildwonders/Shutterstock; 23TC, © iStockphoto/Thinkstock; 23TR, © iStockphoto/Thinkstock; 23BL, © Awe Inspiring Images/Shutterstock; 23BC, © Mike Charles/Shutterstock; 23BR, © Shutterstock.

Publisher: Kenn Goin
Editorial Director: Adam Siegel
Creative Director: Spencer Brinker
Photo Researcher: Brown Bear Books Ltd

Library of Congress Cataloging-in-Publication Data

Green, Jen.
  Sea otter / by Jen Green.
      p. cm. — (The deep end: animal life underwater)
  Includes bibliographical references and index.
  ISBN-13: 978-1-61772-922-5 (library binding)
  ISBN-10: 1-61772-922-1 (library binding)
  1. Sea otter—Juvenile literature. I. Title.
  QL737.C25G7626 2014
  599.769'5—dc23
                          2013011520

Copyright © 2014 Bearport Publishing Company, Inc. All rights reserved. No part of this publication may be reproduced in whole or in part, stored in any retrieval system, or transmitted in any form or by any means, electronic, mechanical, photocopying, recording, or otherwise, without written permission from the publisher.

For more information, write to Bearport Publishing Company, Inc., 45 West 21st Street, Suite 3B, New York, New York 10010. Printed in the United States of America.

10 9 8 7 6 5 4 3 2 1

Contents

Floating and Eating

Not far from **shore**, a sea otter floats in the gentle ocean waves.

It nibbles a clam that it's holding in its paws.

Suddenly, a seagull swoops down.

The hungry bird tries to snatch the tasty food.

In an instant, the otter dives under the waves—still holding its meal.

sea otter

clam

When a sea otter is not diving underwater, it mostly swims or floats on its back.

5

Sea otters are furry **mammals** that live along rocky seashores.

Although they are able to move around on land, they rarely leave the water.

Instead, they stay in the ocean, swimming, diving, and floating.

sea otters floating

Marine Mammals

Mammals that live in the ocean are called marine mammals. Sea otters, dolphins, walruses, sea lions, and killer whales are all marine mammals.

walrus

killer whale

sea lion

dolphins

A sea otter's fur is very thick.

In fact, it is thicker than the fur of any other animal in the world.

The sea otter needs its heavy fur to keep it warm.

The ocean waters that it swims in are very cold all year long.

Where sea otters live

Sea otters live in the northern part of the Pacific Ocean. They swim along the coasts of the United States, Canada, and Russia.

thick fur

What kinds of food do you think a sea otter eats?

Getting Hungry

Sea otters eat small creatures, such as crabs, clams, and mussels.

All these animals live beneath the **surface** of the water.

To catch them, an otter has to dive down into the ocean.

When the water is dark or muddy, it is not easy to see the food.

So an otter uses its paws and long whiskers to feel for its meal.

Sea Otter Food

clams

crab

fish

mussels

Like all mammals, sea otters cannot breathe underwater. However, they can hold their breath for a long time—up to four minutes per dive.

whiskers

paw

Crabs and clams have hard shells. How do you think a sea otter gets to the soft meat inside?

11

A Smashing Meal

Sea otters use their strong teeth to crack the shells of crabs.

However, clams and other animals have shells that are too hard to open this way.

To eat them, a sea otter floats on its back with a rock on its chest.

Then it bangs the clam against the rock.

When the shell breaks, the otter pulls out and eats the meaty part inside.

crab

clam

rock

After eating, a sea otter carefully washes its face and fur.

What kinds of animals hunt sea otters when they are looking for food?

Keeping Out of Trouble

The ocean is a dangerous place for sea otters.

Killer whales and sea lions are their main enemies.

Sometimes, bald eagles catch and eat young sea otters.

bald eagle

killer whales

A sea otter's main way of defending itself is to try to swim away from an enemy.

sea otter

Baby Otters

A baby sea otter is called a **pup**.

For the first few weeks of its life, a pup cannot swim.

Instead, it spends most of its time resting on its mother's belly.

A young pup cannot catch its own food either.

Like all mammals, it drinks milk from its mother's body.

Swimming Lessons

Although a pup cannot swim, it can float very well.

As the pup grows, its mother teaches it how to swim, dive, and catch food.

She also teaches her pup how to lick its fur to keep it clean.

At what age do you think a sea otter can start taking care of itself?

mother

pup

Many sea otters live in places where a kind of **seaweed** called **kelp** grows. A mother otter wraps her sleeping pup in kelp so it will not float away.

kelp

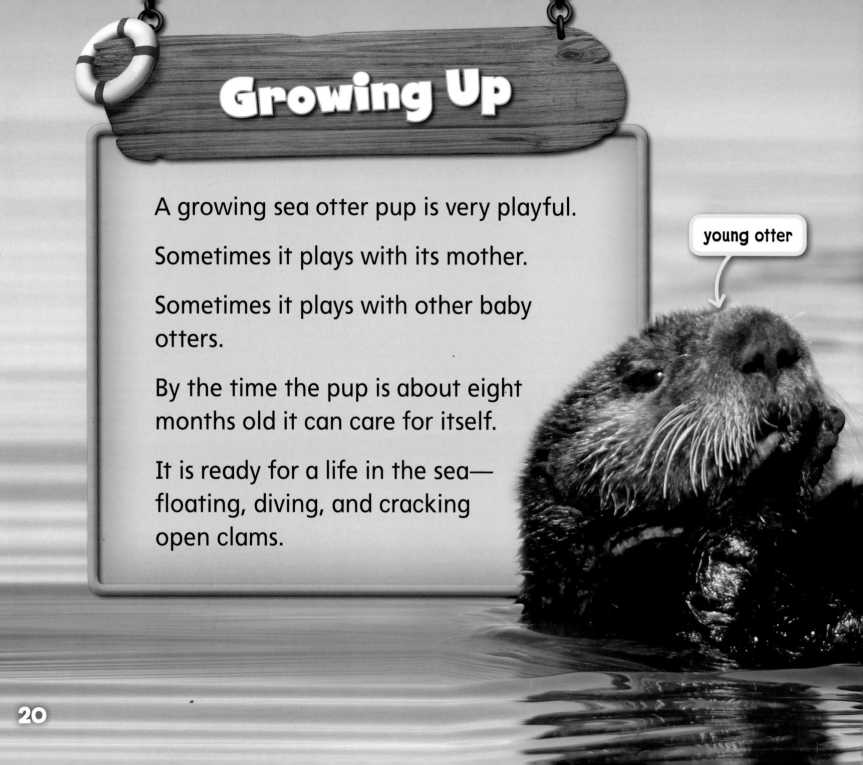

Growing Up

A growing sea otter pup is very playful.

Sometimes it plays with its mother.

Sometimes it plays with other baby otters.

By the time the pup is about eight months old it can care for itself.

It is ready for a life in the sea—floating, diving, and cracking open clams.

young otter

Science Lab

Which Animals Are Sea Otters?

Scientists need to be able to identify different kinds of animals. To do this, they check an animal's color, size, and shape. They also look at things like the shape of its body, paws, and even its teeth.

Imagine you are a scientist who studies sea otters. Look at the pictures on the right. Three of them show sea otters, and three of them don't.

Can you figure out which three pictures show sea otters?

(The answers are on page 24.)

Science Words

kelp (KELP) a type of seaweed that looks like long green or brown ribbons

mammals (MAM-uhlz) warm-blooded animals that have fur and drink their mothers' milk as babies

pup (PUP) a baby sea otter; short for "puppy"

seaweed (SEE-weed) living things that grow in oceans and look like plants

shore (SHOR) the land along the edge of an ocean, river, or lake

surface (SUR-fiss) the top layer of something, such as an ocean or river

23

Index

Read More

Eszterhas, Suzi. *Sea Otter.* London: Frances Lincoln (2013).

Owen, Ruth. *Sea Otter Pups (Water Babies).* New York: Bearport (2013).

Wendorff, Anne. *Sea Otters (Oceans Alive).* Minneapolis, MN: Bellwether Media (2009).

Learn More Online

To learn more about sea otters, visit **www.bearportpublishing.com/TheDeepEnd**

Answers

Pictures A, C, and F are sea otters. B is a killer whale, and D and E are sea lions.

About the Author

Jen Green has been interested in natural history since she was a child. She has written dozens of children's books on subjects as varied as raccoons, gophers, and termites. She loves walking in her native Sussex, England.

Cradlerock Elem. Media Center